I hope you book and would love to talk to you about it!

All my love,
Jodi   2020

780-226-9262
jab8635@gmail.com

Florence Strang

THE BODHISATTVA VOW

JODI LYNN

ILLUSTRATED BY SHENG—MEI LI

The Bodhisattva Vow
Copyright © 2020 by Jodi Lynn

All rights reserved. No part of this publication may be reproduced, distributed, or transmitted in any form or by any means, including photocopying, recording, or other electronic or mechanical methods, without the prior written permission of the author, except in the case of brief quotations embodied in critical reviews and certain other non-commercial uses permitted by copyright law.

tellwell

Tellwell Talent
www.tellwell.ca

ISBN
978-0-2288-3830-2 (Hardcover)
978-0-2288-2832-7 (Paperback)
978-0-2288-2833-4 (eBook)

And a woman spoke, saying,
Tell us of Pain
And he said:
Your pain is the breaking of the shell that
encloses your understanding.
Even as the stone of the fruit must break,
that its heart my stand in the sun,
so must you know pain.
- Kahlil Gibran

In a lonely monk's cell
My story now begins
Of heaven and of hell
Of sainthood and of sin.

I began my life
Sheltered and free
I soared to heights
True love's devotee.

A life of contemplation
And austerity
Patient exaltation
Of Dharma's path and deeds.

Each moment carried
love's sweet song
And I was content
From birth I was hurried along
To love's fulfillment.

There I lived my Karma
"Beloved" I was named
And I fulfilled my Dharma
Peace and love sustained.

*Indeed, it is the meek
Who shall inherit the earth,
And all of those who seek
Shall find their own soul's worth.*

Contentedly, I died there
At last, I came home
Joyfully, I lay there
Peace fully known.

Then, I did meet him
The keeper of heaven's gate
And, I did greet him
At last, to seal my fate.

He said,

"Beloved! It is time
I've opened heaven's door!
Enjoy peace sublime
Be loved forevermore!"

The stage was set, the
line was drawn
Be loved completely now?
But etched within my heart I found
The Bodhisattva Vow!

For I knew beings are numberless
So I vowed to serve them all
Greed and hatred endless
So I vowed to heed love's call.

Dharma's gates are countless
So I vowed to open each one
The Buddha's way is boundless
So I vowed to let perish, none!

*Now indeed, this is where
My story now begins!
To challenge and to dare
The hosts of hell and sin!*

*Though my time had come, yet
I heard an ancient plea
One that I cannot forget
So very easily.*

*I was reborn to end
ignorance and hate
I did sojourn to mend
and open Dharma's gates.*

Dear reader pay attention!
This is a special call
How could I run away from
The greatest love of all?

In each incarnation
It was decreed
I'd help souls find liberation
And nurture love's great seed.

Whatever was needed
I answered love's call
And I always heeded
No matter how small.

Now dear reader, is it clear?
Do you understand?
I am disguised sage and seer
Servant of heaven's hand.

I'm holy trickster! Never late!
I'm sure the angels laughed
I undermined, fear and hate
With clever sleight of hand.

One time I was a prisoner
Reborn, I was a guard
At times appeared a sinner
Reborn, a saint from God!

There was one time, dear reader
That I can recall
One time I was a mangy dog
For a boy so bent and small.

Perhaps there is a special grace
On the other side
Oh, to meet him face to face!
Again, to see him smile!

One time I found a soul
Abandoned and ensnared
Hell's hosts in full control
Alone and in despair.

Then I came, his little girl
To grief so fortified
He thought I was an angel
Beloved! It was I!

Oh, such great compassion!
Furious flames I cooled
Oh, such holy passion!
The hosts of hell I fooled.

Now, dear reader, listen!
To what I have to say
For love it always works
In mysterious ways.

Yes, I was a child
Broken and infirm
But through the breath of heaven
A holy lesson learned.

Indeed, a special lesson!
A family I did greet
The love of heaven resting!
In my crooked hands and feet!

*At times I just came laughing
For souls who never smiled
Oh how my heart was soaring
When love broke through so wild!*

*Sometimes the pain was oh so great
To soul I was midwife
I brought forth love in place of hate
Gratitude and life!*

Dear reader, do you wonder?
Was there a case so bad?
Beyond the reach of heaven?
Beyond mercy's hand?

The thorns, the rocks,
the wayward path
Would sometimes kill love's seed
At times, yes, hell's fervent wrath
Would sometimes thwart my deed.

But Nature does not worry
And never does She cease
Her eyes are always watching
For opportunities.

Deep within each soul
When the soil is ready
Heaven's voice says "go"
My hand so skillful, steady.

Such a far cry!
From solitary life
Such a deep sigh!
Soul's suffering, rife.

I'm love's eternal longing
I'm cleverly disguised
So soul's true belonging
Is finally realized!

But these are not the stories
That I wish to tell
For all of love's fair glories
Were lost to me somehow!

Dear reader, pay attention!
This is a crucial part
Paradise lost; hell's fury won!
A tragic change of heart!

I don't know how it happened
I can only guess
Perhaps, I imagine
An ancient karmic debt.

I have often questioned
What caused me to fall?
What was the lesson?
To learn for one and all.

Perhaps there was a time
When heaven's light flickered
And all I held sublime
Was choked by those who suffered.

In a fateful incarnation
It was decreed
I lost my liberation
And poisoned love's great seed!

Planted in my heart was fear
Oh what a rotten seed!
I blamed God for all held dear
For ceaseless suffering!

Then I laboured diligently
A case for all to see
I waved my fist fervently
Against God almighty!

My fist against heaven's call
My bitterness and rage
For the suffering of all
Life's tormented cage!

Now all of life was suffering
Soul's angry wound I nursed
Life once had been a blessing
Now it had become a curse!

Now among the hated
In the company of famished hosts
I was among the fated
To roam with hungry ghosts!

A wise teacher once asked God
(I don't remember who)
He said, "Please forgive
them Father
For they know not what they do."

Indeed, my master, ignorance
And misery, my handmaiden
Oh, I danced a dismal dance!
Heaven's glory fading.

The holy now forgotten
How the angels must
have shuddered

That seed so rotten!
In stench, decay, mired.

Forgetfulness and misery
They go hand in hand
Fear and ignorance
All led by hell's command.

Such a woeful song did ring
So far from my monk's cell!
Oh how I felt the suffering
In the pit of hell!

Then I began hating
In God, I was disgraced
And I began waiting
To meet God, face to face!

As a panther poised for prey
Self-righteous and determined
For the silent cry of a stillborn babe
I cursed both God and heaven!

Sadly, I did die there
The panther never tamed
Grimly, I did lie there
In hell's torrid flame!

*But Heaven never holds a grudge
And Nature does not weary
How skillfully She moves Her hand
To cool hell's flames and fury.*

Dear reader, I cannot say
Oh, how my soul was burning
But Nature always has Her way
Her Dharma wheels were turning.

Like a potter at Her wheel
So careful and unflawed
A life for me, She did seal
To heal my hate for God!

Once again, called to earth
Again, I was reborn!
This time to souls of great mirth
Compassion love adorned.

Yes, I must commend
These souls were old and wise
Yes, they were, I must contend
Cleverly disguised!

Holy weapons fashioned
Darkness they did rule
Oh such great compassion!
And grace of my gurus!

In my home, I did know
love, grace and bliss
And regularly, I did receive
A Bodhisattva's kiss!

In this incarnation
It was decreed
I'd regain liberation
And nurture love's great seed.

Yet, dear reader, do you see?
This knowledge I bestow
That my soul's past deeds
They follow, like a shadow.

In these days of blessing
Grace undreamed of
In my mother's heart, resting
The eternity of love.

In the wisdom of her heart she saw
That my soul was churning
But in deeper wisdom still she knew
That Dharma wheels were turning.

She said,

"Beloved, our lives have flown
Your time with me is done
Your soul must go, know its own
Work out your salvation!"

"From bitterness and hate
Go find redemption
From soul's wretched state
Fight your battle, win."

In the company of sages
I was raised to heed
The account for my soul's wages
To follow heaven's plea.

It was time to depart
So, I said goodbye
Oh the love of heaven's heart
In my mother's eyes!

The die was cast, the
stakes were high
No turning back, farewell!
In warrior spirit I did cry
I faced my hounds of hell!

My fist against heaven's call
My bitterness and rage
For the suffering of all
Life's tormented cage.

In the end, I did not know
If hell or heaven won
But, dear reader, I could not let go
Or give God pardon.

In the craft of a true warrior
So careful and unflawed
Yet I knew not, what I must do
To heal my hate for God!

Dear reader, I cannot say
Oh how my soul suffered
But Heaven's heart found a way
My anguished cry was heard.

By a master, wise and old
He saw my fear and dread
And the suffering in my soul
He came to me and said:

"I thought I saw you coming
Upon that beaten path
I thought I saw you trying
To lift the holy veil at last."

"Take heart, dear pilgrim,
you're not the first
Nor the last to come
Upon this royal, ancient road
To find liberation."

"But tell me, for I can see
As I look into your eyes
How such a state you've come to be
A soul so old and wise."

"No matter now, dear friend
I see you can't remember
Follow me, to journey's end
To love complete surrender."

Then he washed my hands and face
My sorrow now reprieved
Dharma's path so gentle
And last, he washed my feet.

Oh, such great compassion!
Furious flames he cooled
Oh, such holy passion!
The hosts of hell he fooled!

With love the panther tamed
Sacred medicine
And then my healing came
For this is what he said:

"Sweet pilgrim, do not worry
It's all been said and done
In Heaven's ancient story
None is lost, not one!"

"Please be assured, it is ok
All has been conferred
When darkness is, in full sway
Love has the final word!"

"Remember Him upon the cross
In that place called Calvary
He healed, redeemed,
restored the lost
'It is finished.' Indeed!"

Perhaps to you, my reader
His meanings somehow missed
But to a Bodhisattva's ears
Oh, the joy and bliss!

How could I not remember?
That truth shall set all free!
How could I not surrender?
To love's great mystery!

How could I not have known?
Love always finds a way
And grace is always shown
To the lost and unsaved.

Such grace! It is amazing!
Its sound! So very sweet!
The lost and blind surely!
Will all fall at love's feet!

Even if I kept quiet
I'm sure, without a doubt
In the words of that great Messiah:
"The very stones would cry out!"

Earth's time complete,
lesson learned
Life had taken its toll
And once again I found myself
On heaven's threshold.

Again, I did meet him
The keeper of heaven's gate
Then, I did greet him
At last, to seal my fate.

He said,

"Sweet pilgrim, it is time
To walk through heaven's door
Enjoy peace sublime
Know love forevermore!"

The stage was set, the
line was drawn

It's all or nothing now!
But etched within my
heart, again, I found
The Bodhisattva Vow!

Then I began turning
Away from heaven's door
And I began yearning
For the lonely and the poor.

Even though, I know now
Love always finds a way
Even so, I go now
To the wretched and depraved.

But then I noticed, sagely
A tear fell down his face
And I beheld him, gravely
The keeper of the gate.

Indeed, I cannot express
The drama now unfolding
Such pain, and such distress
That I was beholding.

He said,

"My friend it is my Dharma
To open heaven's door!
And here you've taken cross up!
And wear a crown of thorns!"

"Such love as this bereaves me
How can you defer?
Your actions how they grieve me
And my heart falters."

I said,

"My friend, please don't worry
I hear an ancient plea
And now I must hurry
And perform a noble deed."

"Don't cry for me because
I am sacrifice
My joy, bliss, my ecstasy!
A Bodhisattva's paradise!"

"Remember well the words
From our friend from Galilee
The first is last, the last is first!
Oh do not weep for me!"

"I will come singing, dancing!
Behind the least of these
I will come shouting, laughing!
Holding golden keys."

"For I have tricked the hand of fate
I'll be the last one
To walk boldly through
your golden gate
And find salvation."

And then I washed his
hands and face
His sorrow now reprieved
Dharma's path so gentle
And last, I washed his feet

Then I descended
Into the tentacles of time
And I was contented
In blood, filth and grime.

It does seem, dear reader
We've come full circle now
I long to tell you stories
But they're old and worn, somehow.

Perhaps another time then
When your eyes are new and bright
And the soil within
your tender heart
Is humus, rich and light.

Besides, I am guessing
You've got a lot to do
But perhaps, heaven's blessing
Is resting now on you.

Yes, I must confess
For you I feel affection
For you have been here
with me now
And shared my recollection.

But now my story's over
It's time to go, I guess
But bear with me one moment
And grant my last request.

When you look into your soul
Come friend, do it now!
Do you find love's strong hold?
The Bodhisattva Vow!

*The Bodhisattva Vows are chanted within the
Buddhist community all over the world*

The Bodhisattva Vows

The many beings are numberless; I vow to liberate them

Greed, hatred, and ignorance rise endlessly; I vow to abandon them.

Dharma gates are countless; I vow to wake to them.

Buddha's way is unsurpassed; I vow to embody it fully.

Glossary of Terms

Dharma is a Sanskrit word which simply means "the right way of living." When we live in the right way, we know who we are, and we express the gifts that we have been given. Every person has a purpose in this world. When we fulfill this purpose, we have lived what is known as our Dharma. More importantly, we have learned to be compassionate and to love everybody.

Karma is a Sanskrit word meaning "action" or "doing". Karma is the cycle of cause and effect. Our soul undergoes a long journey before it realizes we are loved and accepted just as we are. We hurt because we have forgotten who we are and why we are put on this earth. Our soul learns through doing and through the consequences of our actions.

CPSIA information can be obtained
at www.ICGtesting.com
Printed in the USA
BVHW020941301020
591459BV00011B/6